Laying On Of Hands

by Derek Prince

"Stir up the gift of God, which is in thee by the putting on of my hands."

II Timothy 1:6

ISBN 0-934920-04-4

TABLE OF CONTENTS

I—TO IMPART BLESSING, AUTHORITY
   AND HEALING   Page 7
   Three Old Testament Precedents -
   Two New Testament Ordinances For
   Healing

II—TO IMPART THE HOLY SPIRIT AND
    SPIRITUAL GIFTS   Page 18
   Helping Believers To Receive The
   Holy Spirit - The Importance Of
   Spiritual Gifts - Example of Timothy

III—TO COMMISSION MINISTERS   Page 28
   Missionaries Sent Out From A Local
   Church - Example Of Paul And Barnabas -
   Deacons Appointed Within A Local Church

DEREK PRINCE

King's Scholar, Eton College
B.A., M.A. Cambridge
Formerly
Fellow of King's College,
Cambridge

ABOUT THE AUTHOR

Derek Prince was born in India, of British parents. He was educated as a scholar of Greek and Latin at two of Britain's most famous educational institutions - Eton College and Cambridge University. From 1940 to 1949, he held a Fellowship (equivalent to a resident professorship) in Ancient and Modern Philosophy at King's College, Cambridge. He also studied Hebrew and Aramaic, both at Cambridge University and at the Hebrew University in Jerusalem. In addition, he speaks a number of other modern languages.

In the early years of World War II, while serving as a hospital attendant with the British Army, Derek Prince experienced a life-changing encounter with Jesus Christ, concerning which, he writes:

> Out of this encounter, I formed two conclusions which I have never since had reason to change: first, that Jesus Christ is alive; second, that the Bible is a true, relevant, up-to-date book. These two conclusions radically and permanently altered the whole course of my life.

At the end of World War II, he remained where the British Army had placed him - in Jerusalem. Through his marriage to his first wife, Lydia, he became father to the eight adopted girls in Lydia's children's home there. Together, the family saw the rebirth of the State of Israel in 1948.

While serving as educator in Kenya, Derek and Lydia adopted their ninth child, an African baby girl. Lydia died in 1975, and Derek Prince married his present wife, Ruth, in 1978.

In the intervening years, Derek Prince has served as pastor, educator, lecturer, and counselor on several continents, and is internationally recognized as one of the leading Bible expositors of our time. He has authored over 20 books, many of which have been translated into other languages. In great demand as a conference speaker, Derek Prince travels frequently to many other parts of the world, and also maintains a base in Israel.

Non-denominational and non-sectarian in his approach, Derek Prince has prophetic insight into the significance of current events in the light of Bible prophecy.

* * * * *

With a few changes, these messages are printed here exactly as they were delivered over the air on the Study Hour radio program.

I
To Impart Blessing, Authority And Healing

Three Old Testament Precedents - Two New Testament Ordinances For Healing

Welcome to the Study Hour.

Our textbook - the Bible.

The study which we shall now bring you is No. 37 in our present series, entitled "Foundations".*

In this series of studies we have been examining the six doctrines which are listed in Hebrews chapter 6, verses 1 and 2, and which are there called "the beginning, or the foundation, of the doctrine of Christ."

The six doctrines which are there listed in order are as follows: No. 1, repentance from dead works; No. 2, faith toward God; No. 3, the doctrine of baptisms; No. 4, laying on of hands; No. 5, resurrection of the dead; No. 6, eternal judgment.

Up to this point we have carefully and systematically examined the first three doctrines in this list. It is now time for us to move on to the fourth of these doctrines - that which is called "laying on of hands".

Had it been left merely to human understanding to decide which are the six basic doctrines of the Christian faith, it is quite probable that this doctrine of laying on of hands would never have been included. However, in the last resort, the best commentary on scripture is provided by scripture itself; and in this particular case, we have the authority of scripture itself for placing this doctrine of laying on of hands amongst the great foundation doctrines of Christianity.

The first 36 studies in this series are published as four successive books, under the titles: "FOUNDATION FOR FAITH"; "REPENT AND BELIEVE"; "FROM JORDAN TO PENTECOST"; "PURPOSES OF PENTECOST". See back cover of this book.

What precisely are we to understand by this phrase, "laying on of hands"? We may answer that "laying on of hands" is an act in which one person places his hands upon the body of another person, with some definite spiritual purpose. Normally this act is accompanied either by prayer, or by prophetic utterance.

Outside the sphere of religion, this act of laying on of hands is not something strange or foreign to normal human behaviour. For example, in some parts of the world, when two men meet who are friends, it is normal for them to lay their hands upon each other's shoulders. This act constitutes an acknowledgment of their friendship, and of their pleasure at meeting each other. Or again, when a mother has a child that complains of headache or fever, it is quite natural - in fact, almost instinctive - for the mother to place her hand upon her child's brow, and in this way to soothe, or to caress, the child.

Within the sphere of religion, the practice of laying on of hands may thus be considered as an extension, or an adaptation, of what is basically a natural human action. As a religious act, the laying on of hands normally signifies one of three possible things. First, the person laying on hands may thereby transmit spiritual blessing or authority to the one upon whom hands are laid; second, the person laying on hands may thereby acknowledge publicly some spiritual blessing or authority already received from God by the one upon whom hands are laid; third, the person laying on hands may thereby publicly commit to God for some special task or ministry the one upon whom hands are laid. At times, all these three purposes may be combined in one and the same act of laying on hands.

If we now turn directly to the Bible, we find that the laying on of hands was already an accepted practice in the earliest records of God's people, as provided by the Book of Genesis. For instance, in Genesis chapter 48, we read how Joseph brought his two sons, Ephraim and Manasseh, to his father Jacob, in order that Jacob might bless them.

In Genesis chapter 48, verse 14, we read: "And Israel (that is, Jacob) stretched out his right hand, and laid it upon Ephraim's head, who was the younger, and his left hand upon Manasseh's head, guiding his hands wittingly; for Manasseh was the first born."

At first, Joseph thought his father had made a mistake, and he tried to make his father change his hands over, placing the right hand upon the head of Manasseh, the first born, and the left hand upon the head of Ephraim, the younger. However, Jacob indicated that he had been conscious of divine guidance in placing his right hand upon Ephraim and his left hand upon Manasseh, and with his hands still kept crossed over in this position, he then proceeded to bless the two boys, giving the first and the greater blessing to Ephraim, and the lesser blessing to Manasseh.

This passage therefore shows plainly that it was an accepted practice that the blessing of Jacob should be transmitted to his two grandsons by laying his hands upon their heads; and, furthermore, that the greater blessing was transmitted through Jacob's right hand, and the lesser through his left hand.

Again, in Numbers chapter 27, we read that as Moses came near to the end of his earthly ministry, he asked the Lord to appoint a new leader over Israel, who should be ready to take Moses' place.

The way in which the Lord ordained that Moses should make provision for this need is recorded in Numbers chapter 27, verses 18 through 20:

"And the Lord said unto Moses, Take thee Joshua the son of Nun, a man in whom is the spirit, and lay thine hand upon him;

"And set him before Eleazar the priest, and before all the congregation; and give him a charge in their sight.

"And thou shalt put some of thine honour upon him, that all the congregation of Israel may be obedient."

The way in which Moses carried out this commandment of the Lord is recorded in verses 22 and 23 of the same chapter:

"And Moses did as the Lord commanded him: and he took Joshua, and set him before Eleazar the priest, and before all the congregation:

"And he laid his hands upon him, and gave him a charge, as the Lord commanded by the hand of Moses."

The result produced in Joshua himself is recorded for us in Deuteronomy chapter 34, verse 9:

"And Joshua the son of Nun was full of the spirit of wisdom; for Moses had laid his hands upon him: and the children of Israel hearkened unto him, and did as the Lord commanded Moses."

From these passages we see that this act of Moses laying his hands upon Joshua was one of great significance both for Joshua himself individually and for the whole congregation of Israel collectively. By this divinely ordained act Moses accomplished two main purposes. First, he transmitted to Joshua a measure of the spiritual wisdom and honour which he had himself received from God; second, he publicly acknowledged before the whole congregation of Israel God's appointment of Joshua as the leader who was to succeed him.

In the latter part of Second Kings chapter 13, we find another example of the laying on of hands as an act of spiritual significance. In the incident here recorded, Joash king of Israel had gone down to pay his last respects to the prophet Elisha, who lay upon his death bed. The following account of that which then passed between Joash and Elisha is given in Second Kings chapter 13, verses 15 through 17:

"And Elisha said unto him, Take bow and arrows. And he (Joash) took unto him bow and arrows.

"And Elisha said to the king of Israel, Put thine hand upon the bow. And he put his hand upon it: and Elisha put his hands upon the king's hands.

"And he said, Open the window eastward. And he opened it. Then Elisha said, Shoot. And he shot. And he said, The arrow of the Lord's deliverance, and the arrow of deliverance from Syria: for thou shalt smite the Syrians in Aphek, till thou have consumed them."

This shooting of the arrow eastward through the window symbolised the victory which Joash was to gain in battle over the Syrians. By this act, therefore, Elisha acknowledged God's appointment of Joash as the leader who would bring deliverance to Israel. This divine appointment of Joash was made effective through Elisha laying his hands upon the hands of Joash, as the latter held the bow and shot the arrow which was symbolical of victory and deliverance. Through the laying on of Elisha's hands, there were transmitted to Joash the divine wisdom and authority needed to equip him as the deliverer of God's people.

This incident is therefore closely parallel to the one in which Moses laid his hands upon Joshua. In each case, this act of laying on hands acknowledged a leader whom God had appointed for a special purpose; and in each case this act also transmitted to that leader the divine wisdom and authority needed to carry out his special, God-appointed task. It is interesting also to notice that, in both cases, Joshua and Joash were appointed primarily as military commanders.

*   *   *

Let us now turn on to the New Testament and see what part this ordinance of laying on of hands plays there. We shall find that there are five distinct purposes for which laying on of hands may be used, according to the precepts and examples of the New Testament.

The first of these purposes is directly associated with the ministry of physical healing. This is stated by Jesus Himself in His final commission to His disciples at the close of His earthly ministry, as recorded in Mark chapter 16, verses 17 and 18. In these verses Jesus appoints five supernatural signs which are to accompany the preaching of the gospel, and which may be claimed by all believers through faith in the name of Jesus. The fifth of these supernatural signs as stated by Jesus is as follows: "In my name . . . . they shall **lay hands** on the sick, and they shall recover."

Here the laying on of hands in the name of Jesus is appointed as a means whereby physical healing may be ministered to those who are sick. Later on in the New Testament another slightly different ordinance is appointed. This is found in the Epistle of James chapter 5, verses 14 and 15:

"Is any sick among you? let him call for the elders of the church; and let them pray over him, **anointing him with oil** in the name of the Lord:

"And the prayer of faith shall save the sick, and the Lord shall raise him up; and if he have committed sins, they shall be forgiven him."

The ordinance here appointed is that of anointing the sick with oil in the name of the Lord.

Both these ordinances alike are effective only through the exercise of faith in the name of the Lord - that is, the name of Jesus. In the case of anointing with oil, it is specifically stated that prayer must accompany this act. In the passage about laying hands on the sick in Mark's Gospel, no specific mention is made of prayer in connection with this act. However, in most cases it would be natural to pray for the sick person, as well as merely laying hands on him.

Again, when anointing the sick with oil, it often seems natural - indeed, almost instinctive - to lay hands upon them at the same time. In this way, the two ordinances become combined in one. However, this need not necessarily be so. It is perfectly scriptural to lay hands on the sick without anointing them with oil. Likewise, it is perfectly scriptural to anoint the sick with oil, without laying hands on them.

The question naturally arises: Is there any difference in use or purpose between these two ordinances - that is, laying hands on the sick, and anointing the sick with oil? Are there times or situations when it is more appropriate to use one ordinance rather than the other? And if so, what are the scriptural principles guiding their use?

The passage in the Epistle of James about anointing with oil begins with the following words: "Is any sick **among you**? Let him call for the elders of the church. . ." Since the Epistle of James is addressed primarily to professing Christians (albeit amongst the Jewish people), the phrase "among you" would seem to refer mainly to Christians. This fits in also with the commandment which immediately follows - "let him call for the elders of the church." A person who made no profession of faith, and was not associated with any Christian church, would not be included in the phrase "among you"; nor would such a person know who were the church elders for whom to send. It would seem therefore that this ordinance of anointing with oil is intended primarily for those who already profess Christianity and are associated with some Christian church.

Interpreted in this way, this ordinance contains two lessons of great practical importance for every professing Christian. First, God expects every sick Christian to seek to Him first, for healing through faith and by spiritual means. This does not mean that it is necessarily unscriptural for a Christian who is sick to seek the advice or help of a medical doctor. But it is absolutely contrary to scripture for any professing Christian who is sick to seek for human medical aid, without first seeking for divine help from God Himself, through the appointed leaders of the church. Today, the great majority of professing Christians who fall sick automatically call for their doctor, without giving any thought to seeking help from God or from the leaders of the church. All Christians who do this are guilty of direct disobedience against the ordinances of God, as set forth in the New Testament. For the scripture says plainly, without any qualification: "Is any sick among you? let him call for the elders of the church. . ." In face of this, any Christian who falls sick, and who thereupon calls for the doctor, without calling for the elders of the church, is guilty of open disobedience. The implications of this act are plain enough, if we pause to consider them. It amounts in effect to saying to God: "God, I do not need you. I do not really believe you can help me or heal me. I am content to accept the best that man can do for me, without seeking to you for guidance or help." This attitude prevailing amongst professing Christians is one main reason why so much sickness also prevails amongst them. For the most part, Christians today have simply set aside the claims of God to heal the body, and have closed the doors of their homes and their churches against Christ the Healer.

The second important lesson contained in this passage from the Epistle of James is that God plainly expects that Christians shall associate themselves with a church, and that the leaders of this church shall be ready to minister in faith, according to the scripture, to the physical needs of their church members. The phrase, "let him call for the elders of the church; and let them pray over him, anointing him with oil in the name of the Lord. . .", plainly carries both these implications: first, that every Christian shall be associated with a church in such a way that its leaders both know him and are known to him; and second, that these leaders shall be ready to minister physical healing to their members in faith, according to the ordinances appointed by God for the church.

In connection with this ordinance of anointing the sick with oil, there are two other points which need to be made plain. First of all, there is no suggestion that oil is to be used because of any natural healing properties that it may possess. Here, as also in many other passages of scripture, the oil is simply a type, or picture, of the Holy Spirit. Thus, placing the oil upon the sick person represents the claim of faith on behalf of that person that the Spirit of God shall minister divine life and healing to his sick body. This claim is based upon the clear promise of God in Romans chapter 8, verse 11: "But if the Spirit of him that raised up Jesus from the dead dwell in you, he that raised up Christ from the dead shall also quicken your mortal bodies by his Spirit that dwelleth in you."

Here the phrase "to quicken your mortal bodies" means to impart divine life and power to the mortal, physical body of the believer in whom the Spirit of God dwells. The great agent of the Godhead who imparts this divine life is the Third Person of the Godhead - the Holy Spirit. This imparting of life to the believer's body by the Holy Spirit is typified by the placing of the oil upon the body. However, it is not the oil itself, but the Holy Spirit typified by the oil, who does the actual work of healing.

The second point which must be plainly stated is that anointing the believer with oil, according to the New Testament, is never intended as a preparation for death, but on the contrary as a way of imparting to the believer the exact opposite of death - that is, divine life and health and strength. Thus, to make anointing with oil a preparation for death is exactly and completely to reverse the true meaning of the ordinance. It is to do just that which God warns against in Isaiah chapter 5, verse 20: to "put darkness for light, and bitter for sweet" - - to put the darkness and bitterness of death and sickness in place of the light and sweetness of life and health.

We may therefore sum up this ordinance of anointing with oil by saying that it is an appointed act of faith by which the impartation of divine life and health through the Holy Spirit is claimed for the body of a sick Christian.

If we now turn back to the other ordinance of laying hands on the sick, as set forth in Mark chapter 16, we shall see that the context there suggests that this ordinance is intended to go together with the preaching of the gospel to the unconverted, and that its primary use is therefore for those who are not yet converted, or who have newly come to the faith. We may form this conclusion from the fact that this, like the other supernatural signs ordained by Jesus, follows immediately upon His commandment to evangelize the whole world, as given to His disciples in Mark chapter 16, verses 15, 16 and 17:

"And he said unto them, Go ye into all the world and preach the gospel to every creature.

"He that believeth and is baptized shall be saved; but he that believeth not shall be damned.

"And these signs shall follow them that believe. . . ."

Jesus then goes on immediately to enumerate the five supernatural signs, ending with the healing of the sick through the laying on of hands. This indicates that each one of these supernatural signs, including the healing of the sick, is intended by God to bear testimony to the divine truth and authority of the gospel message in places where this message has not previously been heard or believed.

This is in line with the account of the disciples' evangelistic activity with which Mark's Gospel closes - that is, in Mark chapter 16, verse 20: "And they went forth, and preached everywhere, the Lord working with them, and confirming the word with signs following. Amen."

This indicates that the primary purpose of these supernatural signs - including the healing of the sick through the laying on of hands - is to confirm the truth of the gospel message amongst people who have not previously accepted it. Therefore it seems clear that the method of ministering to the sick through laying on of hands in the name of Jesus is mainly intended not for established Christians who are members of churches, but rather for the unconverted or for those who have newly come to the faith.

In what way will healing come as a result of the laying on of hands? The scripture does not give any precise or detailed answer to this question. Jesus says merely, "they shall lay hands on the sick, and they shall recover." In place of the phrase "they shall recover", we might translate alternatively, "they shall become well", or more simply still, "they shall be well".

By these words of Jesus two things are still left within the sovereignty of God: the precise way in which healing will be manifested, and the precise length of time that the process of healing will take. Side by side with this, we may set the words of Paul in First Corinthians chapter 12, verse 6: "And there are diversities of operations, but it is the same God which worketh all in all." In this matter of laying hands on the sick there are what Paul calls "diversities of operations". That is, the process of healing does not always operate in the same way each time.

In one case, the laying on of hands may be a channel through which the supernatural gift of healings operates. In such a case, the person who lays on hands by this act transmits the supernatural healing virtue, or power, of God to the body of the one on whom hands are laid; and very often this latter person actually feels within his own body the supernatural power of God.

At other times, however, there is no sensation of power at all, but the laying on of hands is simply an act of naked faith, and of obedience to God's Word. However, if there is genuine faith, the result of healing will follow, even though there may be no dramatic or supernatural experience.

Again, Christ does not specify the length of time that the healing process will take. Sometimes complete healing is received instantly, as soon as hands are laid upon the sick person. At other times, however, healing comes only as a gradual process. In this latter case, it is most important that the person seeking healing shall continue to exercise active faith until the process of healing is complete. It quite often happens that a sick person who is ministered to by the laying on of hands receives a measure of deliverance, but not complete healing. The reason for this usually is that the sick person did not continue to exercise active faith for a long enough period of time to allow the process of healing to be completed. When the person's faith ceases to be active, the process of healing is then arrested. For this reason, it is most important to give scriptural instruction to those seeking healing through laying on of hands, and to warn them in advance of the necessity of holding out in active faith until the process of healing is complete.

Experience has convinced me that in every case where believers lay hands on the sick in the name of Jesus, the process of healing, as promised by Christ, thereupon begins to operate. However, if the sick person then loses faith, the healing is either completely lost, or at best never fully consummated.

There are two main ways in which a sick person may exercise active faith after hands have been laid upon him for healing. The first is by thanking God continually for the measure of healing already received. The other is by refusing to testify any longer to sickness, or to unbelief. People who fail to thank God or to give the right kind of testimony put themselves in a condition where it is almost impossible for God's healing power to continue to operate in their bodies.

*   *   *

In our next studies we shall go on to consider four other scriptural purposes for which the ordinance of laying on of hands may be used.

II
To Impart The Holy Spirit
And Spiritual Gifts

Helping Believers To Receive The Holy Spirit - The Import-
ance Of Spiritual Gifts - Example Of Timothy

Welcome to the Study Hour.

Our textbook - the Bible.

The study which we shall now bring you is No. 38 in our present series, entitled "Foundations".

In this series of studies we have been examining the six doctrines which are listed in Hebrews chapter 6, verses 1 and 2, and which are there called "the beginning, or the foundation, of the doctrine of Christ."

In our last study we began to consider the fourth of the doctrines there listed - that which is called "laying on of hands".

We saw that this ordinance of laying on of hands is recorded in the history of God's people from the Book of Genesis onwards, and that on various occasions in the Old Testament it played a decisive part in shaping the destiny of men and of nations.

In the New Testament we saw that one important use of laying on of hands is to minister healing to the sick, through faith in the name of Jesus. Side by side with this, we also considered the other ordinance appointed in the New Testament for ministering healing to God's people - that of anointing with oil by the elders of the church.

In our present study we shall now go on to consider two further important purposes for which the laying on of hands may be used, according to the precepts and examples of the New Testament.

The first of these two purposes which we shall now consider is to help those seeking the baptism in the Holy Spirit. To form a proper estimate of the part played in this by the laying on of hands, it is necessary to consider briefly all the cases in which the Book of Acts provides us with an account of how people received the baptism in the Holy Spirit. There are altogether five such cases recorded for us in the Book of Acts.

The first case is that of the first disciples in the upper room in Jerusalem on the day of Pentecost. This is recorded in Acts chapter 2, verses 1 through 4.

The second case is that of the new converts in Samaria. This is recorded in Acts chapter 8, verses 14 through 20.

The third case is that of Saul of Tarsus, later the apostle Paul, in the city of Damascus. This is recorded in Acts chapter 9, verse 17.

The fourth case is that of Cornelius and his household. This is recorded in Acts chapter 10, verses 44 through 46.

The fifth case is that of the disciples at Ephesus, to whom Paul preached and ministered. This is recorded in Acts chapter 19, verses 1 through 6.

Anyone who will take time to study these five passages in the Book of Acts will find that, out of five cases where we have a description of people receiving the baptism in the Holy Spirit, in three cases those seeking this experience were ministered to by other believers through the laying on of hands.

In Samaria, the apostles Peter and John laid hands on the new converts and prayed for them; and the record states very clearly, in Acts chapter 8, verse 18, that "through laying on of the apostles' hands the Holy Ghost was given."

In Damascus, the disciple Ananias laid his hands upon Saul of Tarsus that he might receive his sight, and also be filled with the Holy Ghost. In this case, both physical healing and the baptism in the Holy Spirit were ministered to Saul by Ananias through the one ordinance of laying on of hands.

In Ephesus, the disciples to whom Paul there ministered received the Holy Ghost only after Paul had laid his hands upon them.

If we now summarise these facts percentage wise, we may say that in more than fifty percent of the cases in the Book of Acts where people received the baptism in the Holy Spirit, it was through other believers laying hands upon them. Certainly this is not the only way in which people may receive the baptism in the Holy Spirit. In the upper room in Jerusalem and in the house of Cornelius the people there described in both cases received the experience directly, without anyone laying hands upon them. However, on the basis of all the cases considered, we may say that it is both normal and scriptural for those seeking the baptism in the Holy Spirit to be ministered to by other believers through laying on of hands.

It is sometimes suggested that it was only the apostles or special officers of the church who were able to exercise this ministry of laying hands upon other believers that they might be filled with the Holy Spirit. However, this is not supported by scripture. For in Acts chapter 9, verse 10, Ananias, who laid hands for this purpose upon Saul of Tarsus in Damascus, is described merely as "a certain disciple". There is no suggestion that he held any special ministry or office in the church. Yet he was directed by God Himself to lay hands upon the one who was destined to become the great apostle of the Gentiles.

This is in line with what Jesus Himself says in Mark chapter 16, verses 17 and 18: "And these signs shall follow them that believe; In my name . . . they shall speak with new tongues; . . . they shall lay hands on the sick, and they shall recover."

Here Jesus joins closely together the two supernatural signs of speaking with new (or other) tongues, and of laying hands upon the sick for healing, and He says that both these signs alike shall follow (or accompany) the testimony of **"them that believe"**. That is to say, the exercise of these supernatural signs is not confined to any special class of believers, such as apostles, or bishops, or evangelists, or pastors, but is open to **all** "them that believe" - that is, all believers. Just as the scripture leaves open to all believers the ministry of laying hands upon the sick for healing, so the scripture leaves open also to all believers the ministry of laying hands upon other believers that they may receive the Holy Spirit.

However, the scripture also warns us that this ordinance of laying hands upon believers is not to be practised lightly or carelessly. For Paul says to Timothy, in First Timothy chapter 5, verse 22: "Lay hands suddenly on no man, neither be partaker of other men's sins: keep thyself pure."

Here we see that Paul joins together, in this one verse, three distinct warnings to Timothy. The three things concerning which Paul warns Timothy are as follows: first, "lay hands suddenly on no man"; second, be not "partaker of other men's sins"; third, "keep thyself pure".

It is no accident that these two latter warnings follow immediately upon the first warning to "lay hands suddenly on no man." For if this act of laying hands upon another believer - particularly for the baptism in the Holy Spirit - is to be more than a mere religious ceremony, if it is to produce a real spiritual effect, then there must of necessity be a direct spiritual contact between the two believers - that is, the one who lays on hands, and the one upon whom hands are laid. In this contact between two spirits there is always the possibility of spiritual harm resulting to one or both the believers concerned. If the spirit of one believer is not altogether pure - if it is defiled in any way by unconfessed sin, or by evil associations - then there is the possibility that the spirit of the other believer may be harmfully affected by this defiling contact. That this danger is real, is made plain by the two warnings which Paul gives in this particular context: "be not partaker of other men's sins", and "keep thyself pure".

This naturally leads to the question: Since the ministry of laying on of hands is endorsed by scripture, how can we guard against the spiritual dangers connected with it?

The answer is that there are four main safeguards for the believer who desires to exercise this ministry.

First, this ministry should never be exercised lightly or carelessly, but always in a spirit of prayer and humility.

Second, the guidance and direction of the Holy Spirit should be sought at every stage: With whom to pray? When to pray? How to pray?

Third, the believer who lays on hands must know how to claim on behalf of his own spirit the continual purifying and protecting power of the blood of Christ.

Fourth, the believer who lays on hands must himself be so empowered by the Holy Spirit that he is able to overcome any kind of evil spiritual influence seeking to work in or through the one upon whom hands are laid.

Where these four safeguards are not carefully observed, there is a real danger that harmful spiritual results may follow the practice of laying on of hands - either in the one who lays on hands, or in the one on whom hands are laid, or in both. This danger exists in all cases of laying on of hands, but it is greatest in cases where the purpose of laying on of hands is for the baptism in the Holy Spirit. In a figurative way, we may say that the Holy Spirit is heaven's electricity, and the same principle applies in the heavenly as in the earthly realm: the greater the power involved, the greater the need for adequate protection and safeguards.

*　　　*　　　*

The next purpose for the laying on of hands which we shall consider, as set forth in the New Testament, is for the imparting of spiritual gifts. From the passages in the New Testament where this is referred to, it would appear that this particular exercise of the ordinance of laying on of hands is commonly associated with the exercise of the gift of prophecy.

First of all, it is necessary to establish that there is scriptural authority for one believer imparting spiritual gifts to others. This is plainly indicated by the words of Paul to the Christians at Rome, as recorded in Romans chapter 1, verses 11 and 12, where he says:

"For I long to see you, that I may impart unto you some spiritual gift, to the end ye may be established;

"That is, that I may be comforted together with you by the mutual faith both of you and me."

Here Paul says clearly that one reason why he desires to visit the Christians at Rome is that he may thus be able to impart unto them "some spiritual gift". Notice also the effect which this is intended to produce upon the Christians there, for he adds, "to the end ye may be established." In other words, the imparting of spiritual gifts to Christians is one scriptural way of establishing, or strengthening, them in their faith and spiritual experience.

In the next verse, Paul goes on to explain more fully the results of the manifestation of new spiritual gifts amongst the Christians at Rome, for he says: "that is, that I may be comforted together with you by the mutual faith both of you and me." The free operation of spiritual gifts within a congregation enables the various members to comfort, to encourage, to strengthen one another. In this way, not merely would Paul, as a preacher, be ministering to the Christian congregation at Rome; but, through the operation of the spiritual gifts, the members of the congregation would also in their turn be able to minister to Paul. The result would thus be the mutual ministry of the various members to each other.

The operation and the effect of spiritual gifts within a congregation are described by Paul in somewhat similar terms in First Corinthians chapter 1, verses 4 through 8, where he says:

"I thank my God always on your behalf, for the grace of God which is given you by Jesus Christ;

"That in every thing ye are enriched by him, in all utterance, and in all knowledge;

"Even as the testimony of Christ was confirmed in you:

"So that ye come behind in no gift; waiting for the coming of our Lord Jesus Christ:

"Who shall also confirm you unto the end, that ye may be blameless in the day of our Lord Jesus Christ."

Paul here thanks God on behalf of the Christians at Corinth, because they are enriched by God in all spiritual gifts. In particular, Paul specifies the gifts of utterance and of knowledge. Paul also mentions two results which follow from the operation of the spiritual gifts in the Corinthian Church. First, the testimony of Christ is confirmed amongst them. Second, they are themselves confirmed, or strengthened, by God, through these gifts.

Furthermore, Paul indicates that it is the revealed purpose of God that these spiritual gifts shall continue to operate in the Christian church right up to the personal return of Christ for His church. In this connection, Paul uses two phrases, each of which carries the same implication. First he says, "so that ye come behind in no gift, waiting for the coming of our Lord Jesus Christ." Then, in the same context he says again in the next verse, "that ye may be blameless in the day of our Lord Jesus Christ." Both these phrases used here by Paul indicate plainly that the church of Christ at the end of this age will not be considered by God to be complete, or blameless, unless she is fully equipped with all the supernatural spiritual gifts.

In many sections of the Christian church today there is a terrible tendency to treat these supernatural spiritual gifts like some extra chrome fittings, or some fancy gadgets on a car. The suggestion is that the person who wishes to pay a little extra may have the chrome or the gadgets on his car; but that these are not of any real consequence, and the car would really function just as well without them. In the same way, Christians often seem to think that the supernatural gifts are optional - a kind of unnecessary spiritual luxury which people may seek after if they wish, but which are not in any way essential to the proper functioning of the car. However, this attitude is not at all in line with scripture. According to the teaching and examples of the New Testament, the supernatural spiritual gifts are an integral, built-in part of the total car - that is, God's total plan for the Christian church; and without these gifts in operation, the car - that is, the church - can never function on the level of power and efficiency intended by God.

Having thus established the importance of spiritual gifts in the church today, let us now consider what Paul teaches about the way in which spiritual gifts may be imparted. The person to whom Paul refers in this connection is his own co-worker, Timothy.

In First Timothy chapter 4, verse 14, Paul writes to Timothy as follows:

"Neglect not the gift that is in thee, which was given thee by prophecy, with the laying on of the hands of the presbytery."

Again, in Second Timothy chapter 1, verse 6, Paul refers to the same incident in Timothy's spiritual experience, for he says:

"Wherefore I put thee in remembrance that thou stir up the gift of God which is in thee by the putting on of my hands."

In order to complete this picture presented to us by scripture of this particular incident in Timothy's life, we should also take into account the words of Paul in First Timothy chapter 1, verse 18, where he says:

"This charge I commit unto thee, son Timothy, according to the prophecies which went before on thee, that thou by them mightest war a good warfare."

By putting these three passages of scripture together, we are able to establish certain definite facts about the incident here described by Paul.

First of all, Timothy received some definite spiritual gift. The precise nature of this gift is never specified by Paul, and for the purposes of our present study, it is not of any special importance.

Secondly, we learn that this spiritual gift was imparted to Timothy through the ordinance of the laying on of hands. In one passage, Paul says, "with the laying on of the hands of the presbytery." In another passage, Paul says, "by the putting on of my hands."

The word "presbytery" in New Testament is simply a collective noun denoting the elders of a local church. The elders here referred to by Paul may have been those in the church at Lystra, where Timothy began his Christian life, for we read in Acts chapter 16, verse 2, that Timothy "was well reported of by the brethren that were at Lystra and Iconium." Or again Paul may be referring to the elders of the church at Ephesus, where Timothy was when Paul wrote his First Epistle to him. In this case, the same group of elders would be referred to in Acts chapter 20, verse 17, where we read: "And from Miletus he (Paul) sent to Ephesus and called the elders of the church."

Turning back again to Paul's epistles to Timothy, we see that in one place Paul says that it was he himself who laid hands upon Timothy, and in another place he says that it was the elders of the church who did this. Most probably, therefore, Paul acted in conjunction with the church elders. He and they together laid hands upon Timothy.

The third important fact revealed by these passages from the Epistles to Timothy is that the imparting of a spiritual gift to Timothy by the laying on of hands was also associated with prophetic utterance.

In one passage Paul says that this gift "was given by prophecy". This would indicate that the will of God for Timothy to receive this gift was supernaturally revealed through the gift of prophecy; and thereafter the impartation of this gift to Timothy was made effective through the laying on of the hands of Paul and the church elders. In other words, this ordinance of laying on of hands was the means by which the revealed will of God for Timothy was actually made effective in his experience.

In another passage Paul explains a further spiritual purpose for which the prophetic revelation of God's will was given to Timothy, for he says: "This charge I commit unto thee, son Timothy, according to the prophecies which went before on thee, that thou by them mightest war a good warfare . . . "

This indicates that God had a special charge committed to Timothy - a special ministry for him to exercise - a special purpose in life for him to fulfil. The nature of this special ministry was revealed to him in advance - on more than one occasion, it would appear - by prophetic utterances. On one of these occasions it was also revealed that Timothy would need a certain spiritual gift in order to fulfil the ministry committed to him, and on that occasion the particular gift that he needed was imparted to him through the laying on of hands.

Once again, it must be emphasised that this was not a question of the unnecessary or ostentatious use of spiritual gifts. On the contrary, this was something that was vitally necessary to the success of Timothy's ministry. Paul states the purpose for which these prophecies were given to Timothy - "that thou by them mightest war a good warfare."

The Christian life - and especially the life of a minister - is a warfare, a continual contest against unseen forces of darkness and wickedness. These opposing spiritual forces are described by Paul in Ephesians chapter 6, verse 12, where he says: "For we wrestle not against flesh and blood, but against principalities, against powers, against the rulers of the darkness of this world, against spiritual wickedness in high places."

Two main weapons used by these unseen forces of darkness are the weapons of doubt and fear. Doubtless many times in his ministry Timothy passed through periods of great difficulty and opposition, and of apparent failure and frustration. At such periods, he could easily be tempted to doubt the reality of his God-given calling and ministry. For this reason, Paul reminds him of the prophecies which had outlined beforehand God's plan for his life, and he urges him to be encouraged and strengthened by these, so that he may go on to the fulfilment of his God-given task.

In particular, Paul warns Timothy against yielding to fear. For immediately after he has urged him to stir up the gift that is in him by the putting on of hands, Paul goes on to say, in Second Timothy chapter 1, verse 7: "For God hath not given us the spirit of fear; but of power, and of love, and of a sound mind."

What is the remedy that Paul recommends against the insidious attacks of this spirit of fear? The remedy is twofold: first, it is that Timothy should stir up - rekindle into flame - the spiritual gift that he had received through the laying on of hands; second, that Timothy should recall, and be encouraged by, the prophecies that had gone before and had outlined in advance the course that God had planned for his life.

We see therefore, that the ordinance of laying on of hands was combined in Timothy's experience with the gift of prophecy as a means whereby he might be directed, encouraged, and strengthened in the fulfilment of his God-given ministry. According to God's Word, the same means to direct, to encourage, and to strengthen are still available today to God's people, and especially to God's appointed ministers. Furthermore, God's people and ministers still stand in need of these things as much today as in the days of Paul and Timothy.

*   *   *

In our next study we shall go on to consider two more purposes of the ordinance of laying on of hands.

III
To Commission Ministers

Missionaries Sent Out From A Local Church - Example Of Paul And Barnabas - Deacons Appointed Within A Local Church

Welcome to the Study Hour.

Our textbook - the Bible.

The study which we shall now bring you is No. 39 in our present series, entitled "Foundations".

In our last two studies we have been considering the doctrine which is called in Hebrews chapter 6, verse 2, "laying on of hands".

Hitherto we have examined three main purposes for which this ordinance of laying on of hands may be used, according to the teaching and the examples of the New Testament. These three purposes are as follows: first, to minister healing to the sick, through faith in the name of Jesus; second, to help believers seeking the baptism in the Holy Spirit; third, to impart spiritual gifts.

We saw that the exercise of this ordinance of laying on hands is not restricted to any special class of people, such as apostles, or bishops, but is open to all true believers who possess the necessary spiritual qualifications. In all cases, however, the ordinance of laying on of hands should always be exercised in a humble and prayerful spirit, subject to the leading of the Holy Spirit and to the spiritual safeguards indicated in the Word of God.

In our present study we shall now go on to consider two further important purposes for which the laying on of hands may be used.

The first purpose of the laying on of hands which we shall now consider is connected with the sending out of Christian workers from a local church. The church which is set forth in the New Testament as an example of this is the church at Antioch, in Syria; and the passage in which this use of laying on of hands is described is found in Acts chapter 13, verses 1 through 4:

"Now there were in the church that was at Antioch certain prophets and teachers; as Barnabas, and Simeon that was called Niger, and Lucius of Cyrene, and Manaen, which had been brought up with Herod the tetrarch, and Saul.

"As they ministered to the Lord, and fasted, the Holy Ghost said, Separate me Barnabas and Saul for the work whereunto I have called them.

"And when they had fasted and prayed, and laid their hands on them, they sent them away.

"So they, being sent forth by the Holy Ghost, departed unto Seleucia; and from thence they sailed to Cyprus."

This passage gives us a great deal of extremely interesting information about the way in which, according to the New Testament, a local church conducted its affairs.

First of all, we notice that in this church at Antioch two definite spiritual ministries were present, and were recognised by the church. These two ministries were those of the prophet and the teacher. Within the congregation five men were recognised and mentioned by name as exercising these particular ministries.

Secondly, we notice that these leaders in this congregation not merely prayed, they also fasted. Furthermore, they did not merely fast privately as individuals, but they fasted together in a group.

This in line with the prophetic exhortation for the last days, given to us through the prophet Joel, in Joel chapter 1, verse 14: "Sanctify ye a fast, call a solemn assembly, gather the elders and all the inhabitants of the land into the house of the Lord your God, and cry unto the Lord."

And again in Joel chapter 2, verse 15: "Blow the trumpet in Zion, sanctify a fast, call a solemn assembly. . ."

After these exhortations to united fasting by God's people, there follows, in Joel chapter 2, verse 28, the promise of the outpouring of the Holy Spirit: "And it shall come to pass afterward, that I will pour out my Spirit upon all flesh. . ."

We know that this prophecy of the outpouring of the Holy Spirit upon all flesh received its initial fulfilment on the day of Pentecost and in the experience of the early church; and that in our day, once again, a similar outpouring of the Holy Spirit upon all flesh, but on an even greater scale, is being reenacted right around the world. The early church received "the former rain" of the Holy Spirit, as promised in Joel chapter 2, verse 23. Today we are experiencing "the latter rain", as promised in the same verse.

Since the promise of the outpouring of the Holy Spirit is for us in these days, it is only logical to acknowledge that the exhortations to united fasting, which come earlier in the same prophecy of Joel, are also for us. It would be quite illogical to apply the exhortations to fasting to some past or future age, while reserving the actual outpouring of the Holy Spirit for the present. In actual fact, the whole context of Joel's prophecy makes it plain that periods of united fasting and prayer are one main preparation which God's people should make, if they wish to enter into the fulness of the outpouring of the Holy Spirit upon all flesh, as promised by God for these last days. In this connection, the prophecy of Joel lays special emphasis on the leaders of God's people. In Joel chapter 1, verse 14, it specifies "the elders"; and in Joel chapter 2, verse 17, it specifies "the ministers of the Lord". Thus the spiritual leaders of God's people are called upon to set a public example in this matter of fasting.

Clearly the leaders of the church at Antioch understood the matter in this way, for the passage which we have already read, in Acts chapter 13, verse 2, states: "they ministered to the Lord, and fasted."

What was the outcome of their waiting upon God with fasting in this way? This is recorded in the same verse: "the Holy Ghost said, Separate me Barnabas and Saul for the work whereunto I have called them." One reward which they received for thus waiting upon God was that the Holy Ghost spoke directly to them and in this way revealed to them the mind and purpose of God for the extension of His work through them. The phrase, "the Holy Ghost said. . ," indicates that the words following, "Separate me Barnabas and Saul. . .," are the actual words spoken by the Holy Ghost. In the light of other New Testament teaching on the operation of the gifts of the Holy Spirit, it is reasonable and scriptural to suppose that the Holy Spirit spoke on this occasion through a human instrument, either by the gift of prophecy, or by the gifts of tongues and interpretation.

It is important to notice the exact words here used by the Holy Spirit: "Separate me Barnabas and Saul for the work whereunto **I have called them.**" The verb "I have called" is in the perfect tense. This indicates that God had already spoken privately and individually to Paul and Barnabas about the work that He wanted them to do, before He spoke publicly concerning them and their work to all the leaders of the church. Thus, the words spoken by the Holy Spirit publicly to the group of leaders were both a revelation and a confirmation of the call which Paul and Barnabas had already received directly and privately from God. Since Paul and Barnabas were both mentioned by name in the public utterance of the Holy Spirit, it is plain that this utterance was not given through either of them, but through one of the other men then present.

How did these men react to this supernatural revelation of God's will? This is described in the next verse - Acts chapter 13, verse 3: "And when they had fasted and prayed, and laid their hands on them, they sent them away."

Notice that they did not immediately send Paul and Barnabas off on their God-appointed mission. First, they set aside further time for fasting and prayer. This was the second time that they had fasted and prayed together. Through their first period of prayer and fasting they received the special, supernatural revelation of God's plan. Then, in their second period of prayer and fasting, it is reasonable to suppose that they united together to claim on behalf of Paul and Barnabas the divine grace and power which they would need for the accomplishment of God's plan.

Thereafter, the sending forth of Paul and Barnabas from the church at Antioch was consummated by one further ordinance. The other leaders of the church laid their hands upon Paul and Barnabas, and so sent them forth.

What was the precise nature of the ministry for which Paul and Barnabas were in this way commissioned and sent forth? In contemporary Christianity, the title usually given to Christian workers thus sent forth from a local church is "missionaries". However, the actual word used in the New Testament is "apostles".

This becomes apparent if we compare the phraseology used in Acts chapter 13, verse 1, with that used in Acts chapter 14, verses 4 and 14. In Acts chapter 13 Paul and Barnabas are described as "prophets and teachers". In Acts chapter 14 they are called "apostles". The word "apostle" means literally "one sent forth". Thus this title was applied to Paul and Barnabas after they had been "sent forth" from the church at Antioch.

By its origin the word "missionary" likewise means "one who is sent". Thus the words "apostle" and "missionary" have the same original meaning. However, in modern Christianity the word "missionary" is applied in many cases where it would not be scriptural to use the word "apostle". Since it is outside the scope of our present study to examine the precise nature and extent of the apostolic ministry, it will be sufficient to use the more generally accepted word "missionary", with the understanding that in this study it can be applied only to missionaries who are called to a ministry of an apostolic nature.

What was the significance of this ordinance of laying on of hands, as here described in the sending forth of Paul and Barnabas from the church at Antioch?

First of all, it represented the open, public acknowledgment by the church leaders of the fact that God had chosen and called Paul and Barnabas to a special task and ministry. Secondly, by laying hands upon Paul and Barnabas, the other church leaders claimed for them the special spiritual wisdom, grace and power which they would need for the successful accomplishment of their God-given task.

In this respect, this use of laying on of hands here in the New Testament is closely parallel to the incident already referred to in the Old Testament, where Moses laid hands upon Joshua, and in this way publicly acknowledged God's choice of Joshua as the leader who was to succeed him, and also imparted to Joshua the spiritual wisdom and authority needed for his God-appointed task.

God's own summary of the process by which Paul and Barnabas were appointed and sent forth as missionaries from the church at Antioch is given in the next verse, Acts chapter 13, verse 4: "So they **being sent forth by the Holy Ghost,** departed unto Seleucia."

Notice that phrase, "being sent forth **by the Holy Ghost.**" The church at Antioch, with its leaders, were the human instruments by which God revealed and worked out His will for the sending forth of these two missionaries. But behind and through these human instruments, there operated the wisdom, the foreknowledge, and the direction of the Holy Spirit Himself. In the final analysis, it was He, the Holy Spirit Himself, as the executive agent of the Godhead now present here on earth, who was responsible for the commissioning and sending forth of these two missionaries. In the whole procedure here followed at Antioch we find a perfect example of divine and human cooperation - God and His church working as partners together.

Let us now consider briefly what was the outcome of this first missionary journey of Paul and Barnabas, thus entered into by the direction of the Holy Spirit, with prayer and fasting, and with the ordinance of laying on of hands.

This is recorded for us in Acts chapter 14, verses 26 and 27:

"And thence (they) sailed (back) to Antioch, from whence they had been recommended to the grace of God for the work which they fulfilled.

"And when they were come, and had gathered the church together, they rehearsed all that God had done with them, and how he had opened the door of faith unto the Gentiles."

There are three points of interest to notice here.

First, we are here given an authoritative, scriptural account of the purpose for which the church leaders had laid their hands upon Paul and Barnabas. We are told that, by this ordinance, Paul and Barnabas had been "**recommended to the grace of God for the work.**" Thus, this use of the ordinance of laying on of hands constitutes a means by which God's servants may be recommended to the grace of God for a special work to which God has called them.

Second, we must observe the outcome of the labour of Paul and Barnabas. The scriptures states that "they **fulfilled**" their God-given work. This means that they completely and successfully accomplished their work, without omissions or failures. Someone has said: "God's callings are God's enablings." In other words, when God calls a man to a special task, God also makes available to that man all the means and the spiritual grace required for the complete and successful accomplishment of that task.

Third, we should notice the impact of their ministry upon the Gentiles. The scriptures states: "God...had opened the door of faith unto the Gentiles." Paul and Barnabas did not beat against a closed door. Wherever they went, they found that God had gone before them, to open the doors and to prepare the hearts. Such is the power of united prayer and fasting: to open doors that otherwise would remain closed. The power thus generated by prayer and fasting was made available to Paul and Barnabas, according to the needs that lay before them, through the ordinance of laying on of hands.

In this connection, I would add my own conclusion, based on a varied experience as a minister and a missionary in many different lands. My conclusion, briefly, is this: New Testament results can be achieved only by New Testament methods.

*   *   *

It remains to consider one further use, recorded in the New Testament, of the ordinance of laying on of hands. This use is somewhat similar to that which we have just examined. It is recorded in Acts chapter 6, verses 1 through 6:

"And in those days, when the number of the disciples was multiplied, there arose a murmuring of the Grecians against the Hebrews, because their widows were neglected in the daily ministration.

"Then the twelve called the multitude of the disciples unto them, and said, It is not reason that we should leave the word of God, and serve tables.

"Wherefore, brethren, look ye out among you seven men of honest report, full of the Holy Ghost and wisdom, whom we may appoint over this business.

"But we will give ourselves continually to prayer, and to the ministry of the word.

"And the saying pleased the whole multitude: and they chose Stephen, a man full of faith and of the Holy Ghost, and Philip, and Prochorus, and Nicanor, and Simon, and Parmenas, and Nicolas, a proselyte of Antioch:

"Whom they set before the apostles: and when they had prayed, they laid their hands on them."

Here we have an account of the appointment of seven men to an administrative office in the church at Jerusalem. By the common consent of almost all interpreters, it is agreed that the office to which these men were appointed was that which came to be designated by the official title of "deacon". We find that the appointment of these men as deacons was made effective through the laying on of hands by the church leaders.

In order to understand this procedure more clearly, it is necessary to analyse briefly the structure of leadership in the local church, as set forth in the New Testament. We find that this basic structure was extremely simple. It consisted of two - and only two - classes of administrative officers. These two classes were "elders" and "deacons".

To those who are familiar only with the King James version of the New Testament, it might appear that there are, in addition to "elders" and "deacons", two other classes of church officers - namely, "bishops" and "over-seers". However, a closer examination of the actual words used in the original Greek will reveal that this is not so. In actual fact, the three titles "bishop", "overseer", and "elder", are merely three different names for one and the same office. ·

The English word "bishop" is derived, with a few small changes, from the Greek word "episkopos". The plain, literal meaning of this Greek word "episkopos" is "over-seer". Sometimes the King James version renders the word as "overseer"; at other times it renders it by "bishop".

For example, in Acts chapter 20, verse 28, and in First Peter chapter 5, verse 2, this Greek root "episkopos" is translated by the English words "overseer" and "over-sight". On the other hand, in Philippians chapter 1, verse

1, in First Timothy chapter 3, verse 2, and in Titus chapter 1, verse 7, the same Greek word "episkopos" is translated by the English word "bishop". No matter which word may be used in translation, each alike describes one and the same office. If we desire the plainest and most literal translation of the Greek word "episkopos", undoubtedly this would be "overseer".

Again, the examination of these and other New Testament passages reveals clearly that the title "elder" denotes precisely the same office as that of "bishop" or "overseer".

For example, in Acts chapter 20, verse 17, we read that from Miletus Paul "sent to Ephesus, and called the **elders** of the church." A little further on - in verse 28 of the same chapter - we read that Paul said to these men: "Take heed therefore unto yourselves, and to all the flock, over the which the Holy Ghost hath made you **overseers**. . ." Thus, by putting these two verses together, we learn that the two titles "elder" and "overseer" denoted one and the same office.

Again, in Titus chapter 1, verse 5, Paul writes to Titus: "For this cause left I thee in Crete, that thou shouldest set in order the things that are wanting, and ordain **elders** in every city, as I had appointed thee. . ."

In verse 7 of the same chapter, Paul goes on to describe the qualifications which an elder should possess, and he says: "For a **bishop** must be blameless, as the steward of God. . ." In other words, Paul uses the two words "elder" and "bishop" interchangeably to describe one and the same office.

Thus we find that these three words "bishop", "overseer" and "elder" are merely three different titles used to designate one and the same office. Probably the most commonly used title for this office is that of "elder".

In addition to the "elders", we find, as already stated, the "deacons". Apart from these two - elders and deacons - no other administrative officers of the local church are recorded in the New Testament.

The main qualifications for these two offices are set forth in the following passages of scripture: Acts chapter

6, verse 3; First Timothy chapter 3 throughout; Titus chapter 1, verses 5 through 9.

Upon the basis of these passages, we may summarise the main features of these two offices as follows. The primary task of the elders is to give spiritual direction and instruction to the church. This is indicated by the words of Paul in First Timothy chapter 5, verse 17: "Let the elders that rule well be counted worthy of double honour, especially they who labour in the word and doctrine." Here the two main duties of elders are described as "ruling" and as "labouring in the word and doctrine".

On the other hand, the primary task of the deacons is to minister in a practical way to the material needs of the congregation. This is summed up in Acts chapter 6, verse 2, by the brief phrase to "serve tables".

In the early chapters of the Book of Acts there is no account of how the elders of the church in Jerusalem were appointed. However, later examples of such appointments made by Paul and Barnabas would indicate that it was the apostles who had the responsibility of appointing elders in each local church; and there is no reason to doubt that this is what happened originally in the church at Jerusalem.

When we turn on to the record of the ministry of Paul and Barnabas, we find that part of their responsibility was to appoint elders in the local churches which they had established. For example, in Acts chapter 14, verse 23, we read that Paul and Barnabas ordained elders in every one of the new churches that they had planted. Again in Titus chapter 1, verse 5, Paul directs Titus to "ordain elders in every city."

Neither here, nor anywhere else, is there any suggestion that elders were appointed either by election, or with the ordinance of laying on of hands.

On the other hand, the procedure for appointing deacons is outlined in Acts chapter 6, verses 3 through 6. Here we find that the apostles delegated to the congregation as a whole the responsibility for choosing from amongst their own number men suited to fill the office of deacon. After these men had been chosen by the congregation, they were brought before the apostles, who first prayed over them, and then laid hands upon them.

This act of laying hands upon these deacons served three main purposes. First, the apostles publicly acknowledged thereby that they accepted these men as fitted to hold the office of deacon. Second, they publicly committed these men to God for the task for which they had been chosen. Third, they transmitted to these men a measure of their own spiritual grace and wisdom needed for the task that they had to carry out. In this connection, it is interesting to notice that two of these men appointed as deacons - Stephen and Philip - subsequently developed outstanding spiritual ministries of their own.

*   *   *

In closing this study, we may enumerate the five main purposes indicated in the New Testament for the laying on of hands. First, to minister healing to the sick; second, to help those seeking the baptism in the Holy Spirit; third, to impart spiritual gifts; fourth, to send out missionaries; fifth, to ordain deacons.

In order to understand these five uses of laying on of hands, we have been led to examine in some detail the pattern of daily life and administration of a local church, as revealed in the New Testament.

If we now sum up the lessons learned in our three studies that have been devoted to the laying on of hands, we see that this ordinance has a close and vital connection with many important aspects of the Christian life and ministry. It is directly connected with the ministry of healing; with the equipping of believers for active witness through the baptism in the Holy Spirit; and with the commissioning of specially called Christian workers. It is often associated with the gift of prophecy. It also strengthens the life of the local church in two ways: spiritually, through the impartation of spiritual gifts; and practically, through the appointment of deacons.

For all these reasons, the ordinance of laying on of hands logically takes its place, in Hebrews chapter 6, verse 2, among the great foundation doctrines of the Christian faith.

*   *   *

In our next studies in this series we shall go on to consider the next great foundation doctrine of the Christian faith - that is, "the resurrection of the dead". *

*The last thirteen studies in the "Foundations" series are contained in Book VI "RESURRECTION OF THE DEAD" and Book VII "ETERNAL JUDGMENT". See back cover of this book.

MESSAGES AVAILABLE ON CASSETTE

SPIRITUAL CONFLICT ALBUM I

1001	How Conflict Began: The Pre-Adamic Period
1002	The Rebellion of Lucifer
1003	Results Produced by Lucifer's Rebellion
1004	The Adamic Race: Five Unique Features
1005	Adam's Fall and its Results
1006	Results of Adam's Fall (cont'd)

SPIRITUAL CONFLICT ALBUM II

1007	Jesus The Last Adam
1008	The Exchange Made at the Cross
1009	Jesus Tasted Death in all its Phases
1010	The Cross Cancelled Satan's Claims
1011	Jesus the Second Man
1012	God's Purpose for the New Race

SPIRITUAL CONFLICT ALBUM III

1013	Five Ways Christ Undoes Satan's Work
1014	God's Program for the Close of the Age—Part I
1015	God's Program for the Close of the Age—Part II
1016	Satan's Program for the Close of the Age
1017	Restraining And Casting Down Satan
1018	Spiritual Weapons: The Blood, The Word, Our Testimony

EFFECTIVE PRAYING

4001	Seven Basic Conditions for Answered Prayer
4002	Intervening By Prayer in National Affairs
4003	Fasting Precipitates God's Latter Rain
4004	Spiritual Weapons For Spiritual Warfare
4005	God's Atomic Weapon: The Blood of Jesus
4006	Epilogue: The Glorious Church

PROPHECY

7001	Climax in four phases: Repentance, Refreshing, Restoration, Return of Christ
7002	Divine Destiny for this Nation (USA) and this generation
7003	Prophecy: God's Time Map
7004	Israel and the Church: Parallel Restoration

- **Each Message is approximately one hour in length.**
- **A printed verse-by-verse analysis and outline is included with every tape.**